HOW TO STOP

OVERTHINKING

A PRACTICAL GUIDE TO BREAKING THE CYCLE OF WORRY AND ANXIETY

MARY FRANKLIN. C.

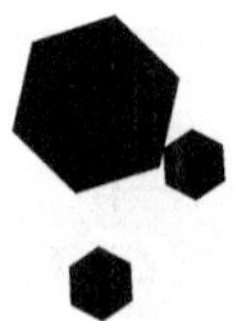

DEDICATION

To All of My Admired Readers, "How To Stop Overthinking: A Practical Guide To Breaking The Cycle Of Worry And Anxiety" is a book that will help you find who you are. With that, I offer you my sincere gratitude and a warm hug.
Your choice to begin this life-changing journey is a testament to your bravery and dedication to leading a happy and prosperous life. These remarks contain profound advice and useful tactics, but they also serve as a bright light of optimism amid the clouds of uncertainty.
This book is a tribute to the human spirit's tenacity and the limitless potential that every one of us possesses.

I cordially invite you to completely engage with the lessons and exercises provided here, dear reader.
Allow each page to act as a gentle reminder of your intrinsic value and the seemingly endless opportunities that lie beyond fear. Recognize that you are never alone and embrace the trip and the process.
But this is merely the beginning of our trip; it does not finish here. I implore you to share your experiences with others as you forge ahead on your path of strength and self-discovery. Your voice has raised, inspired, and sparked change in the lives of those who surround you.

As you approach the last chapter of this book, I would like to ask you one last favour, you kindly consider posting a review so that other seekers might benefit from your ideas and insights? Your advice is really helpful and can be a beacon of hope for those who are following in your footsteps.
I sincerely appreciate you allowing me to join you on this life-changing adventure. I hope you find serenity, fulfilment and purpose in your life by following the advice that these pages have to offer.
With unending love and appreciation, [Mary Franklin. C.]

COPYRIGHT © 2024
MARY FRANKLIN. C.

This Covers has been designed
From Freepik.com

TABLE OF CONTENTS

Love and care more about your children, especially when they are facing any problem, always be there for them, and support them.

This helps to strengthen the bond between parents and their kids. Let love lead the way

INTRODUCTION

Overthinking is a very big problem that needs urgent care and response. Millions of people around the world have been victims of the problem in one way or the other, because of certain problems that they may be facing in their different locations.

The act of Overthinking can cause enormous damage to the human brain since it's associated with mental problems. Moreover, it's vital to note that mental health disorders, including those exacerbated by overthinking, can contribute to a variety of negative outcomes, including suicide, substance abuse, and physical health problems. If you or someone you know is struggling with overthinking or any other mental health issue, it's advisable to seek support from qualified professionals such as therapists, counsellors, or psychologists. Breaking free from overthinking can be quite as easy as you think, but need to work harder, discipline yourself, and try as much to live a healthy life. An adage says that health is wealth.

Do you want to be among those who keep on suffering from the problem now and then? No! I guess that should be your answer. Overthinking itself is not typically a direct cause of death or destruction; rather, it's often associated with mental health issues such as anxiety and depression, which can have serious consequences if left untreated.

As someone who has struggled with thinking too much, I can share my path to break free from its crushing grip.

The tendency to overthink was like being caught in my labyrinth, where each thought led to the next, resulting in an endless cycle of worry and anxiety. It arose from a deep dread of making mistakes, not being good enough, and the uncertainty looming around every turn.

Overthinking has several reasons, including perfectionism and nervousness about failure, as well as prior traumas and unresolved emotions.

For me, it was a combination of societal pressure-induced perfectionism and a proclivity to linger on past events, examining every little thing in search of significance and approval.

The repercussions of overthinking were significant and far-reaching.

 It deprived me of priceless moments of delight and spontaneity, rendering me frozen by indecision and obsessed with self-doubt.

 Insomnia, migraines, and a continuous knot in my stomach were the physical manifestations of my incessant mental chatter.

If left uncontrolled, overthinking may become a vicious cycle, resulting in increased stress, worse decision-making, and, eventually, burnout. It's like being trapped in a maelstrom, where the more you resist, the deeper you fall into despair.

But, despite the darkness of overthinking, there is always a ray of hope. For me, the watershed moment came when I recognized that overthinking was not a sign of intelligence or diligence, but rather a hindrance to leading a full life. I searched for credible knowledge and practical techniques, using reputable sources such as psychological studies and expert advice.

Through mindfulness practices, cognitive behavioural therapy, and self-compassion exercises, I learned to quiet my mind's constant chatter and embrace the present moment with open arms. I found that the ultimate magic is not in controlling every outcome or forecasting every twist and turn, but in submitting to the ebb and flow of life with grace and acceptance.

CHAPTER ONE
UNRAVELING THE WEB OF OVERTHINKING

When faced with an important choice, which might involve attending university, changing occupations, purchasing a car, or marrying or divorced, most people consider all possible outcomes. It therefore makes an awful lot of sense. A substantial cost or life change requires careful, detailed analysis.

However, it may be difficult for you to stop repeating certain concepts in your mind. You may obsess over even little decisions and think about what-ifs to the point of paralysis. Experts refer to the phenomenon as overthinking.

It is frequently encountered to get too "in your mind" at times. However, prolonged thinking too much can begin to disrupt your sleep, job, health, interpersonal relationships, and other elements of your daily life. Do you suspect you may be a person who overthinks? This is what you ought to be aware of.

What exactly does it imply when we overthink?

Consider your mind to be a lively marketplace, with traders selling their items and thoughts competing for attention. Overthinking is akin to becoming trapped in this chaotic marketplace, helpless to manoeuvre through the noise and chaos. The continual replaying of circumstances, the infinite "what-ifs," and the obsessive examination of every detail all contribute to an endless cycle of anxiety and worry.

Overthinking, additionally referred to as rumination, happens when you continuously focus on a specific topic or circumstance until it impairs your life. Excessive thinking typically breaks down into two categories: concentrating on past events and fretting concerning what's to come.

If you suffer from excessive thinking, you might feel "stuck" or unwilling to take any steps at all. It is occasionally challenging to clear your mind and pay attention to other things.

Thinking too much can produce anxiousness, but not all tension is negative. In the near term, possessing a great deal of ideas about a distressing issue can motivate you to take action.

When you're apprehensive about a significant position presentation, for instance, that stress can motivate you to take action.

It may motivate you to work diligently on the project and arrive promptly on the day of the presentation to guarantee that you are on time. Overthinking can also help you be aware of what you stand for and potential opportunities for personal growth.

"Not all overthinking is harmful," Mary Franklin explains. On the other hand, it becomes problematic when it keeps you from making an effort or disrupts your routine and happiness.

What are the indicators of thinking too much?

We all get hooked on particular ideas or anxieties from time to time. Recognizing that something is taking place is an initial step toward addressing it.

Signs of thinking too much or rumination include:

1. Concentrating on the same ideas, anxieties, or fears repeatedly.
2. Imagine worst-case situations.
3. Repetition of having a bad experience from the past
4. Spending an extensive amount of time contemplating negatively about the previous or tomorrow.
5. Feeling gloomy or dissatisfied because of what you have to say
6. Concentrating on a topic is so overwhelming that you are unable to concentrate on other things.
7. Continuing to consider a situation after you have previously discovered plausible options.
8. Inability to proceed on to the next crucial issue due to your keep brooding on the same problem.

Why do we tend to overthink things?

According to Mary Franklin, a neuropsychologist in New York City, thinking too much can be a means of attempting to manage a situation and gain confidence in what to do next. When you overthink, your brain tries to lessen your worry by running through several situations and predicting what will happen.

However, when we overthink, we frequently become trapped in this state and struggle to move forward and take action. "The trouble with thinking too much is that our minds nearly always come up with new anxiety questions," Mary Franklin explains.

Studies contend that a few persons are more receptive to ruminating than other a set of individuals. The tendency to overthink is common among idealists.

"Individuals who are perfectionist and successful have a tendency to overthink things due to their apprehension of failure and the urge to be flawless, which ends up replaying or critiquing decisions and blunders," explains Mary Franklin.

Is thinking too much regarded as a psychological problem?

The process of overthinking isn't regarded as a disorder of the mind in and of itself. Nevertheless, research has discovered that it is commonly an early sign of multiple mental health problems, such as:
1. Depressive disorder
2. anxiety-related conditions
3. Obsessive-Compulsive Disorder (OCD)
4. Post-traumatic Stress Disorder (PTSD)
One study discovered a two-way link between introspection and anxiousness. Mary Franklin. C. refers to it as a "chicken-and-egg" scenario: excessive levels of anxiety, nervousness, and sadness can all result in ruminating over. In the meantime, worrying can give rise to additional nervousness, anxiety, and sadness.

Different kinds of Overthinking

Professionals do not categorize thinking too much into "classifications." However, certain individuals overthink by using cognitive biases. Cognitive biases are erroneous structures of perception that frequently cause stress, worry, and despair.
Several types of mental errors are:
1. All-or-nothing: Seeing things consistently one way or another, with no middle ground in between.
2. Catastrophizing: Consider the worst potential conclusion in an instance.
3. Exaggerating: Assuming that things will always be the same way based on very few examples.
4. Rushing to conclusion: Considering you are familiar with something will end out without sufficient proof.
5. Reading minds is a conviction that you understand what an individual thinks without necessary proof.

Make friends and share your problems
with them, it's a cool way of relieving
yourself from Overthinking.

Procedure To Stop Yourself From Overthinking

We have a wide range of methods you can help yourself and your mind from thinking too much, especially about a particular problem. Moreover, techniques like taking deep breaths, and asking for help from close friends and a medical healthcare professional will play a big role in relieving the stress of thinking too much.

Hazardous patterns of thought

You ultimately obtain a few peaceful moments to yourself, but you immediately wonder if you neglected to write that gratitude email or if you misjudged your odds of earning the promotion.

Sounds familiar? Being worried and thinking too much are natural parts of our lives, but they can hurt our well-being if not managed properly.

According to 2021 research, focusing on the same ideas could boost your chance of developing certain mental health issues.

So, what should a person who overthink do? These suggestions can point you in the correct path.

1. Take a step back and consider your response.

The way you react to your thoughts might occasionally trap you in a cycle of rumination, or recurrent thinking. Rumination can often lead to unpleasant outcomes. Trusted source for a person's mental health.

Take note of how your mood changes the next time you find yourself constantly replaying things in your head. Do you experience irritability, nervousness, or guilt? What is the predominant emotion driving your thoughts?

Having self-awareness is essential for changing your thinking.

2. Create a way to get distracted.

Engage in an enjoyable hobby to avoid overthinking.

This appears differently for everyone, but examples include:

Learning new kitchen abilities by attempting a new recipe. Attending your favourite workout class.

Consider starting an exciting activity, like creating art, or helping with a neighborhood charity.

It is occasionally difficult to pick up something exciting while your thoughts are racing. If finding a diversion seems difficult, attempt to set aside a brief period — say, thirty minutes. — each day. Use the moment for yourself to investigate potential detours or participate in existing ones.

3. Take deep breaths.

You've heard it hundreds of times before, but it works. When you find yourself flipping back and forth over the ideas you're thinking, close your eyes and take a long breath.

Try it.

Here's a fantastic beginner activity to help you calm down while taking a breath:

Find an appealing spot to sit and rest on your shoulders and neck.

Put one palm over your heart, the other in your tummy.

Inhaling and exhaling using your nose, concentrating on noticing how your chest and belly move throughout your take in oxygen.

Try the act on three separate occasions every day for a total of five minutes, or whenever your mind races.

4. Meditate

Setting up frequent sessions of meditation is a procedure based on cleansing yourself of restless chatter by focusing inward.

All you'll require is five minutes and a peaceful area.

5. Looking at the big picture.

How could the issues currently on your conscience influence you in 5 or 10 years? Will anyone notice that you purchased a fruit dish for the potluck rather than preparing a pastry from scratch?

Don't let tiny concerns evolve into major obstacles.

6. Do something pleasant for somebody else.

Trying to alleviate another person's load can help you gain insight. Determine how you can assist a person who is going through a difficult moment.

Does your friend amid a divorce require a few days of child care? Can you bring up provisions for your ailing neighbour?

Realizing you can brighten someone's day can help keep negative thoughts at bay. It also provides you with something constructive to concentrate on instead of your never-ending stream of ideas.

7. Try to navigate automatic negative thoughts (ANTs).

Automatic negative emotions are knee-jerk unfavourable sentiments that occur in response to a scenario and are frequently associated with fear or anger.

Tackling ANTs

You can recognize and collaborate over your ANTs by writing down your ideas and actively striving to modify them:

Use a journal to record the scenario causing you nervousness, how you are feeling, and the first thing that comes to mind.

As you delve into the facts, consider why the scenario is creating these negative feelings.

Break down your feelings and try to figure out what you're believing yourself about the scenario.

Find an alternative to your initial idea. For instance, rather than saying, "This will prove to be an incredible failure," say, "I'm honestly trying my best."

8. Recognize your achievements.

When you notice yourself thinking too much about anything, take out a notebook or use the best note-taking software on your phone. Make a list of five positive things that have happened in the last week, along with your role in them.

These don't have to be major successes. Perhaps you stayed within your coffee allowance this past week or cleared out your car. When you examine it on print or screen, you may be amazed at how many small details build up.

If it helps, refer to turn in this list when your thoughts are swirling.

9. Stay present.

Not prepared to dedicate yourself to a meditation practice? There are plenty of other strategies to stay grounded in the current moment.

Be here now.

Here are some ideas:

1. Unplug. Turn off your device of choice for a set period of uninterrupted time each day and devote that time to a single task.

2. Eat mindfully. Pamper yourself to a few of your most beloved dinners. Try to find joy in each bite, and concentrate on the way the food smells, tastes, and feels in your mouth.

3. Get outside. Take a stroll outside, even though it is only a fast lap around the block. Take note of anything you notice along the trip, such as smells or sounds.

10. Consider various perspectives.

Sometimes quieting your thoughts means moving outside of your regular perspective. Your life experiences, values, and assumptions affect your perspective on the world. Imagining things from a different perspective can help you sort through some of the noise.

Take notes on some of the ideas that are running through your mind. Try to figure out how valid each one is. For example, maybe you're worried about an impending vacation because you know it will be a disaster. But is this truly going to happen? What kind of evidence do you have to back this up?

11. Take action!
You could find yourself repeating the same sentiments because you are not taking actionable steps to deal with a certain circumstance.
Can't cease thinking over a person you envy? Instead of letting it destroy your day, use your emotions to assist you in making better decisions.
The next time the green-eyed monster visits, be active and jot down ideas for how to achieve your goals. This will help you get out of your brain and focus your energy on taking actionable steps.
12. Practice compassion for oneself.
Concentrating on previous errors prevents you from letting go. If you're beating yourself up over anything you did last week, try concentrating on self-compassion.
Here are a few ideas to get you started:
Make note of a worrisome idea.
Pay attention to any emotions or physical responses that arise.
Recognize that your feelings are valid for you right now.
Adopt a phrase that resonates with you, such as "May I accept myself as I am" or "I am enough."
13. Accept your fears.
A few things are forever beyond your control. acquiring knowledge to deal with this can help reduce overthinking. One 2018 study by Trusted Source found that admitting troubling ideas and fears can aid enhance psychological well-being.
Of course, this is simpler compared to doing, and it will not occur overnight.
However, look for tiny chances to deal with the circumstances you regularly worry about. Maybe it's stepping up to a pushy colleague or making that long-awaited solo day trip.
14. support request.
You don't need to make it alone. Obtaining appropriate therapy from a trained professional could assist you build new methods for processing your ideas and even alter the way you think.

CHAPTER THREE

RACING THOUGHTS: HERE'S WHAT YOU OUGHT TO DO WHENEVER YOUR MIND RACES.

When you succumb to racing thoughts, you may face difficulties such as insomnia and insufficient sleep. Treatment may include easy home breathing exercises as well as longer-term options like prescription and prevention.

Having racing thoughts are rapid and persistent mental process. They could be overbearing. Such ideas could revolve around one particular subject or comprise numerous distinct paths of thinking. You may have feverish fantasies about a money-related situation, a discouraging experience, or a dread. Such notions may also spread.

Brain racing might heighten feeling worried or awkward and compromise your capacity to sit down and concentrate.

When your emotions are rushing, you may experience things like:

1. Your mind is racing.
2. You are unable to calm down what you are thinking.
3. Your mind is unable to "shut off," therefore you cannot relax.
4. It's impossible to focus on other things.
5. You remain anxious over a situation that has grown beyond control.
6. You begin to catastrophize or consider worst-case circumstances.

Insomnia can be the outcome of a racing mind. This occurs when you are unable to fall asleep because your thoughts are racing. Continue reading for information about ways to calm yourself down, long-term therapy decisions, and what's driving your mind to race.

How to prevent the brain from racing thoughts

When you are going through worrying thoughts, you can take numerous measures to moderate or prevent them:

1. Concentrate on breathing.

Take a few deep, deliberate breaths, counting each inhale and exhale. This can make your mind concentrate on anything besides your frantic thoughts. It can alleviate the brain and spinal cord. This can assist in alleviating anxiety.

Some soothing breathing patterns may include:

4-7-8- Breathing: box breathing, diaphragmatic breathing, alternate nostril breaths.

Continue reading: Learn more about breathwork.

2. Try a mantra.
To distract yourself from rushing thoughts, repeat a mantra as needed. Even a statement like "Everything will be OK" can be useful. Mantras can assist reduce tension, fear, and depression.
3. Reduce tension before sleeping.
If your frantic thoughts happen at night when you try to sleep, modify the way you go to bed to allow you to unwind and rest comfortably.
Try to avoid anxiety for at least two hours before sleeping. You can meditate or do light yoga, enjoy a book or newspaper, or relax in a bubble bath. Minimize all technological devices and mentally mentally active two hours before bedtime.
Therapy
Continued treatment may be useful in determining the source of your racing ideas. Cognitive behavioural therapies (CBT) may be especially helpful. It can give you adaptive methods and strategies for dealing with these ideas.
Such methods could include:
Performing prolonged inhalation activities.
To minimize stress, try writing down your ideas, utilizing mantras, and focusing on what you can manage right now.
Medications for managing whirring ideas Someone with medical training might suggest medicines assisting handle deeper conditions particularly if worries appear to follow triggers such as phobias or bipolar episodes. Drugs like these may consist of:
1. Antidepressants.
2. nervousness medicines
3. mood boosters
What results in racing thinking?
Having a constant racing idea in your mind could represent an indication of a variety of diseases. While it is predominant in nervousness, other mental health issues can also trigger racing emotions. Anxiety Tension often generates anxious feelings. Having racing thoughts is very frequent throughout a stressful event, but they may happen at any moment. They can take place before or following an episode of anxiety.
ADHD
ADHD is defined by a trend of apathy or excitement. Some people report a lack of attention as rapid thinking, particularly when confronted with external stimuli. Wandering thinking, or the inability to concentrate on just one path of belief, may be uncommon in ADHD.
Obsessive-compulsive disorder Obsessive-compulsive disorder (OCD) is a wellness difficulty noted for constant cravings or addictions. These interests might manifest as rapid thinking when you are unable to stop what appears to be an avalanche of ideas about a specific subject. You may have a habit that calms your mind, for instance, scrubbing your hands a specific set of times to alleviate the worrying induced by germ-related nervousness.
Bipolar disorder.
Bipolar disorder is a cognitive of the mind whereby one's feelings encompass tremendous heights (anxiety) to lowest points (sadness). Brainstorming behaviours are common throughout frenzy scenes, but they can also occur in depression, especially agitated sadness.

Agitated depression.

Anxious despair is an old speech for an intense form of sorrow. It is distinguished by feeling agitated rather than lethargic, which is often linked with nearly every kind of grief. You could additionally feel: Anxious, agitated, and eager to respond. Agitated people with anxiety may be more prone to encounter frantic ideas than people who have various kinds of melancholy.

Medication side effects

Medication may occasionally cure specific signs of an illness while exacerbating or causing other symptoms. Medicines utilized for the relief of anxiety, sadness, or bipolar disorder can occasionally create restless sadness, which can result in frantic thinking. If you begin taking a new medicine and experience racing thoughts, contact your doctor as soon as feasible so that you can try a different prescription or change your dosage.

When to call for medical attention

Look into seeing a doctor or psychologist if you're experiencing erratic ideas on a regular schedule that are disturbing or keep you from sleeping. If you have erratic emotions and any of the signs that follow, you should see a counsellor as soon as feasible to be examined for an illness or psychological issues.

1. warning signs of melancholy.

2. strong restlessness.

3. Strong compulsions.

4 . Anxieties.

5. nervousness cause drastic mood changes. Once you've received your diagnosis, you can begin psychotherapy. Disorders of the mind, like other medical issues, are simpler to deal with when noticed beforehand.

Unity is strength, never fail to help people in need, especially your friends who cloud their minds with unnecessary thoughts

Chapter Four

Six Daily Solutions for Overcoming High-Functioning Anxiety.

If you searched "overachiever" in the dictionary, you'd probably see my picture where the definition should be. I grew up in a Washington, D.C. suburb and am a product of the city's hectic pace.

And, during my working career, I have done well in every position I have held. I was usually the first person to show up and the last to depart the office. My lists of tasks were the most orderly and color-coded.

I am a team player and an organic social speaker, and I know exactly what I need to say or do to please those around me. Sounds ideal, right? Except 99.9 per cent of my coworkers and managers didn't realize that I also lived with generalized anxiety disorder. Anxiety affects approximately 19%Trusted Reference of older people in the USA each year.

While other people are paralyzed by nervousness, I am propelled at a million miles per hour. My type of anxiety is "high-functioning," which means that my signs are concealed by overdoing, thinking too much, and overperforming.

For many years, I didn't realize working so diligently and caring so much was wearing me out. They appeared to be positive features rather than signs of a condition, which is why identifying them is so challenging. "No matter how difficult I worked or how pleased I was with my successes, the anxious portion of my brain scrutinized, criticized, and patronized me."

And, saddest of all, I grieved in silence. I did not tell my coworkers or managers. My dread of judgment and misinterpretation was too great.

The simplest way to figure out how to cope with what was happening was to try harder and never give up. For the first decade of my profession, anxiety drove me through highs and lows. A few years ago, I found myself amid a significant mental health crisis.

Thanks to medication, counselling, and a lot of hard work, I've come to embrace and own the fact that I have high-functioning anxiety.

Today, I identify my ways of thinking and acting and apply practical strategies to step in when I find myself drawn into the worry vortex. The items that follow the six life tips are based on my experience.

1. Understand your ailments as they are. "I approach my anxiety as if it were a bodily problem, as psychological conditions are also bodily. This reduces my concern regarding what I was feeling at the time of passing.

Do you grasp the manifestations of high-functioning anxiety? If not, learn to know them. If you do, consider and realize how they affect you. Anxiety causes our brains to become overly analytical. "Why, why am I feeling this way?" Sometimes the reason is simple: "Because we have anxiety." Ruminating over a simple decision, over-preparing for a meeting, or worrying over a conversation are often just symptoms of my anxiety.

Mood disorders are partly natural, and I try to take care of my anxiety like any other medical problem. This enables me to stop worrying about how I'm feeling at the moment. I tell myself, "I have anxiety, and that's fine." I may embrace that this morning is slightly challenging and instead focus my attention on where I can assist myself.

2. Make buddies with your fears. If you are anxious, terror is your buddy. You may dislike it, but it is a part of your existence. And it inspires much of what you do. Have you examined regardless of your fear? Have you correlated it to previous events that may have taught you that you aren't smart or accomplished enough? Why are you so fixated on the approval of others?

Anxiety, in my opinion, cannot be ignored or avoided. With the support of a therapist, I was able to confront my phobia. Rather than adding to my anxiety, I attempted to figure out what led to it. For example, I can recognize that my nervousness stems from my want to be liked and accepted, rather than from delivering a fantastic presentation. This realization has reduced part of its influence over me.

3. Get acquainted with your body. "I take walks outside on a lunch hour. I exercise. I practice yoga. When I'm feeling too busy or overwhelmed... I do these events anyway. Given that I want them, even if only for 10 or 15 minutes."

Anxiety is both emotional and physical. Those with severe anxiety tend to remain in their minds, making it difficult to interrupt the loop of frightened thinking and feelings. I used to devote 10 to 12 hours every day at the office and never exercised. I felt stalled, both in my body and my mind. Getting back in touch with my body is a vital element of how I cope with my symptoms now.

I practice taking deep breaths all day, every single day. Whether I'm in a conference, working on my laptop, or driving home in traffic jams, I can take deep, deliberate breaths to increase oxygen circulation, relax my muscles, and reduce my blood pressure. I stretch at my desk. I take walks outside on my lunch break. I exercise. I practice yoga. When I'm feeling too busy or overwhelmed... I do these kinds of things anyway. Since I want them, even if only for 10 or 15 minutes. Having a good interaction with my body helps me get out of my brain and redirects my restless energy in a constructive direction.

4. Create an affirmation and recite it daily. I've learned to talk back to my fears.
When the not-so-little voice within tells me that I'm not good enough or that I
need to push myself harder, I've devised a few mantras to counter it: "I'm satisfied
with who I am right now." "I'm doing my best." "I'm not perfect, but I love myself for
who I am."
"I need to take monitor myself." This approach is particularly insightful in coping
with a difficult sign of high-functioning nervousness: perfectionist behaviour.
Having a mantra empowers me and allows me to exercise self-care while still
coping with my anxiety. I realize that I have a voice and that what I require is
essential particularly when it comes to my well-being.

5. Learn to intercede with yourself. "When I start obsessively checking back and
forth, I stop. I remove myself from situations that increase my anxiety. Anxiety
feeds off of itself, like a massive snowball moving downward. Once you've
identified your symptoms, you may learn how to respond when they arise and
move out of the way before you're rolled over.
I find it tough to make judgments, whether they are about developing a brochure
or selecting a brand of dishwasher detergent. When I start obsessively checking
back and forth, I stop. I force myself to walk away from whatever is causing my
anxiety to rise. One tool I use is a timer. When the timer goes off, I hold myself
accountable and walk away. If I've had a very stressful week at work, I don't follow
it up with a busy weekend. This may entail saying "No" and disappointing someone,
but I need to prioritize my health. I've discovered hobbies outside of work that I
find relaxing, and I schedule time for myself to accomplish them.
Understanding how to modulate my moods and actions in reaction to anxiety has
helped me manage my symptoms and reduce my overall stress.

6. Form a backup squad. One of my greatest anxieties was alerting others at work
about my anxiety. I was frightened to tell everyone around me that I was afraid -
what a bad mental loop! I'd get stuck in a black-and-white reasoning cycle,
informing either no one or everyone. However, I've now discovered that there is a
healthy balance.
I contacted a few coworkers with whom I felt comfortable. When you're having a
horrible day, being able to talk to one or two people might be quite beneficial. This
relieved a lot of strain off of me because I wasn't pushing through each day with a
superhuman persona of positivity.

Creating a small support group was the first step toward being a more true version
of myself in both my professional and personal life.
I also discovered that being open worked both ways, because my coworkers
immediately approached me, making me feel quite good about my decision to open
up. All six of these life hacks can be combined to create a highly powerful anxiety
toolbox. Whether I'm at work, at home, or out with friends, I can utilize these
techniques to put myself back in control. Learning to manage anxiety takes time,
which can be stressful for Type A personalities. However, I am convinced that if I
devote even a fraction of that overachieving energy to my well-being, the
outcomes will be positive.

Overthinking Can be painful, always try as much as
possible to ease your mind from those awful thoughts

Chapter Five

Trauma, either temporary or long-term, influences individuals in numerous manners. This is likely not news to you. But did you understand that four distinctive answers can assist clarify how your encounters influence your response and behaviour? First, there is fight-or-flight, which you are presumably most familiar with. In simple terms, when confronted with an imminent danger, you either oppose, react in kind, or run.

You may also have seen this alluded to as flight, fight, or freeze. The freeze reflex is similar to stalling in that it provides a brief pause for the mind and body to organize and get ready for the next steps. However, the reaction to trauma might extend beyond flight, fight, or freeze. Therapist Mary Franklin invented the word "the fawn reaction." which denotes (occasionally unconscious) action that seeks to please, placate, and soothe the danger to safeguard oneself from additional harm.

We'll go over all of these trauma responses thoroughly below, in addition to providing some context for why they arise and tips for understanding (and navigating) your unique experience.

First, let's look at the essentials. As you may well acknowledge, trauma responses occur naturally. When your body detects an emergency, the cerebellum and autonomic nervous system (ANS) activate rapidly, unleashing chemicals such as cortisol and adrenaline.

These hormones cause bodily modifications which aid you get ready for an imminent danger, whether it is bodily, psychological, or imagined harm.

You may, for example: dispute with a coworker who is treating you unfairly. To avoid a conflict, follow these tips: leave a motorist running a red light, freeze upon hearing an unexpected disturbance in the dark, and keep your emotions to yourself.

It is also possible to experience an overactive trauma response. In a nutshell, this means that everyday occurrences and events that most people do not see as threatening might activate your default stress reaction, which could be a fight, flight, freeze, fawn, or a hybrid.

Hyperactive trauma responses are rather prevalent among trauma survivors, specifically individuals who have suffered long-term abuse or neglect. In reality, an excessive trauma response—being locked in fight, flight, freeze, or fawn—can occur as an aspect of post-traumatic stress disorder (PTSD) or complicated post-traumatic stress disorder (C-PTSD).

How does bonding come into play here? Your attachment type reflects your formative relationship with your parents or primary provider of care. This initial connection shapes how you engage with others throughout your entire life. If your caregiver met your basic requirements and you could rely on them for emotional and physical assistance, you likely grew up with a willingness to trust others and form positive connections with friends and lovers.

You will also, according to Mary Franklin"s theory, be able to weather stress, obstacles, and other risks by utilizing the trauma reaction that works best in a specific situation. Living through recurrent neglect, exploitation, or other forms of trauma in childhood could render you find it hard to use these reactions successfully.

Living through recurrent neglect, exploitation, or additional trauma in childhood might make it difficult to use these responses successfully. Instead, you may find yourself "stuck" in one mode, coping with conflict and obstacles in the same way you did as a child:

1. Select the reaction that best meets your requirements by allowing you to avoid more pain.

2. This undoubtedly complicates the task of developing good partnerships.
Example Say you desire to shield the younger ones from your parent's rage and aggressiveness. You do not want to flee and leave them alone. However, you are aware that you must take action in some way, so freezing is out. This leaves two choices: To prevent a violent outburst from a parent, either fight or pacify them.

You might possess an instinctive liking for one over another according to your underlying character qualities, but the circumstances can also influence this. If you can't think of a subtle way to respond to your parent's size and strength, you may resort to fawning. If the answer is effective, it can simply become routine in all your relationships, even years later.

Now let's take a closer glance at the four major responses.

The fight response

This behaviour stems from the subconscious notion that keeping your authority over others leads to the affection, affection, and safety you seek but did not receive as a child.

 This behaviour seems to appear more frequently when your caretakers:

1. Do not provide appropriate and healthy boundaries.

2. Gave you what you requested for

3. shame you exhibited

4. selfish behaviour, such as wrath, bullying, or disdain.

While fighting commonly corresponds to actual physical or emotional aggressiveness, it can involve any action you take to stand up to or eliminate a threat, such as:

1. Examples of illicit conduct include making a public social media post after a cheating partner. 2. Shouting at a friend.

3. Spreading rumours about a coworker.

4. Refusing to communicate with your partner for a week after they lose your sunglasses.

According to Mary Franklin C., narcissistic defences can be based on a fixed fight response. Indeed, doctors accept childhood maltreatment as a possible aetiology of this disorder, nevertheless, other elements may play a role. In relationships, you could show more uncertain or avoiding connection types.

Flight reaction

In a nutshell, a flight action is defined by the urge to avoid or deny pain, mental upheaval, and other forms of hardship. You may find yourself locked in flight mode if, as a child, avoiding your parents allowed you to avoid the majority of their maltreatment and mitigate the impact of the cruelty that you suffered. Escape may take a literal form:

1. Spending more time at school and with colleagues.
2. In addition to exploring the area.

Or in a more figurative sense:
1. To stay occupied, engage in studies, plot escapes, and
2. Use music to block out disagreements.
As an adult, you may continue to avoid tough situations by:
1. Striving for perfection in all aspects of life.
2. Ending relationships when threatened.
3. Avoiding conflict, and using work, hobbies, or alcohol to cope with fear, anxiety, and nervousness.

FThe freeze reaction

The freeze action is a stalling technique. Your brain clicks the "stop" button but stays constantly watching and observing meticulously so it can decide if fleeing or fighting is a better option for safety. Some specialists were quick to point out that this reaction occurs before you decide whether to leave or fight. And what if either course of action appears to be impractical? You may then "flip" in response to your fear.
What is the flop response? Your body can become limp. You could detach or faint, which may appear advantageous to you at the moment. 1. If you pass out, you don't feel the trauma directly.
2. If you split up, you may feel alienated or socially disengaged from the situation, or you may not remember it completely.
3. If you go limp, the individual hitting or abusing you may use less force or lose interest altogether. As a result, you may find it easier to reach safety.

Of course, flopping (also known as tonic immobility) isn't always a pleasant thing, but it serves a purpose. It can render you utterly numb, preventing you from moving or calling for aid. Furthermore, while it may appear beneficial to have no memories of abuse, such blank gaps can nonetheless create mental suffering.
Long-term freeze anticipation may look like a mask worn to safeguard oneself when no other means of fighting back or fleeing are apparent. Behind the mask, you could:
1. Use fiction or creative thinking to get away from daily stress.
2. I like isolation to prevent tight interactions. hide your emotions and sentiments.
3. To detach from the world, try sleeping or staying in your room.
4. You can also mentally "check out" from uncomfortable or distressing circumstances.

The fawn responds.

Mary Franklin C. uncovered a fourth trauma reaction while working with survivors of childhood abuse and trauma. This response, which he described as "fawning," provides an alternative road to safety. In summary, you avoid damage by learning to please and satisfy the individual who is threatening you. In childhood, this may involve:

1. When looking after a parent, it's necessary to put first their preferences, build your character, and offer praise and respect, even if they criticize you.
2. You would develop the ability to fawn, for instance, to satisfy a narcissistically protected mother or father or one whose conduct is unreliable.
Giving up personal boundaries and limits in infancy may have helped to reduce abuse, but this behaviour typically persists into adulthood, fueling codependency or people-pleasing tendencies.
1. You may Accept your partner's requests, even if it means refraining from continually praising management to avoid unfavourable feedback.
2. feel as if you know very little about what you like and appreciate. In close relationships, it's common to avoid discussing personal ideas or sentiments for fear of causing anger.
3. Additionally, there may be a lack of boundaries around one's own needs.
The lasting impact of trauma Trauma doesn't only affect you in the moment. More commonly, it has long-term repercussions that can affect well-being for years to come. Even a single episode of maltreatment can inflict tremendous anguish and trauma. Persistent maltreatment can have even more disastrous effects, compromising your ability to build good interpersonal connections, as well as your physical and emotional health. But you can triumph over trauma and reduce its influence on your life.

Being aware of your trauma sensitivity is a great spot to begin. Please keep in mind that your comment may not fit perfectly into any of the four aforementioned groups. According to Mary Franklin's idea, most persons who experience long-term trauma develop a hybrid reaction, which involves fawn-flight or flight-freeze.
Therapy can frequently be essential While relations with loved ones may continually aid with trauma and abuse wellness, most people require extra encouragement. In truth, PTSD and C-PTSD are well-known psychological wellness illnesses that rarely resolve without expert help.
With aid from a mental state specialist, you may either: Break out from a fixed trauma response and gain knowledge to respond with greater efficiency to real-world threats. Start healing emotional trauma while acquiring the ability to set appropriate boundaries. Get acquainted with the feeling of self.

The bottom line .

Your trauma response could be a residue of a difficult upbringing, but it is not permanent. A qualified psychologist will aid you tackle the long-term repercussions of past trauma, as well as any emotional problems which may occur as the outcome.

CHAPTER SIX

What is the link between trauma and anxiousness?

Trauma and anxiousness have a close link. Stressful events might put the mind in a state of survival, always on guard and anticipating.

Trauma arises when you participate in or witness a negative event that takes over your stress reaction and cognitive ability to cope. Situations that might trigger trauma consist of conflict, catastrophes of nature, assault, watching passing away and life-threatening accidents.

It is normal to encounter a variety of feelings following a traumatic occurrence, such as anger, remorse, despair, and confusion. These sentiments are determined by the type of your encounter, your level of involvement, and how the situation impacts your belief system.

It is normal to encounter a variety of feelings following a traumatic occurrence, such as anger, remorse, despair, and confusion. These sentiments are determined by the type of your encounter, your level of involvement, and how the situation impacts your belief system. Anxiety is a frequent symptom across all trauma themes because of its participant stress response, generally recognized as the "fight, flight, or freeze" reaction.

How can trauma result in anxiousness?
Trauma is an unappealing encounter resulting in discomfort. It naturally leads to unsavoury ideas and emotions such as despair, rage, and fear. When you've been through anything terrible worried over it recurring over and over and alleviating the anguish might cause anxiousness.

However, the correlation connecting trauma and anxiety extends beyond simple cause and effect. Anxiety is not inherently evil. It is a component of your body's response to stress, which is a series of bodily functions which take place when your brain detects a problem. Temporary anxiety is a sign of increased attentiveness and consciousness. You are aware of the impending adversity and are prepared for it. Anxiety disappears as the imagined danger disappears in an average stressful situation. However, the nature of trauma can keep anxiousness from disappearing. Trauma is an episode that reflects mental overwhelm. It can induce long-term psychological and structural alterations in your brain, locking you into "fight, flight, or freeze" mode. Constantly sensing a threat might cause anxiety.

Persistent worry caused by unpleasant recollections is only one side of the equation. Experiences of trauma can also alter how the mind senses dangers. According to research, trauma hinders the amygdala, the brain region in charge of activating survival mode, from distinguishing between current and past threats. This means that recalling past trauma might cause the same amount of fear as if the experience were occurring in the present.

Is anxiousness following trauma generally linked with post-traumatic stress disorder?
Anxiousness may arise following trauma without matching the standards of diagnosis for post-traumatic stress disorder (PTSD) or any nervousness condition. Prolonged anxiety from trauma can cause disorders of anxiety such as PTSD, however just a small percentage Source: People who have experienced trauma acquire PTSD. Doctors define anxiety disorders as caused by trauma when signs are prolonged and ubiquitous, causing severe impairment in everyday activities.

Signs of trauma-related anxiousness.

Trauma-related anxiousness could look different from one individual to another. The seriousness of the symptoms varies, and not everybody suffers from them all. It is possible to have one or two main signs, such as those linked to PTSD, but not fulfil the standards for diagnosis. Some instances of trauma-related symptoms of anxiousness are:
1. Stay away from individuals, places, and things that evoke memories of the terrible incident. 2. Remembering the events through flashbacks or dreams disturbing recollections.
3. Constantly worrying about what happened and feeling nervous or hypervigilant.
4. Increasing heart rate, perspiration, or shortness of breath when you remember about the stressful encounter.

5. Panic attacks. Symptoms may include difficulties falling asleep, trouble staying focused, anxiousness, nausea, headache, and persistent discomfort.
6. Crying frequently

What are your ways of dealing with trauma-related anxiety?
What you have gone through is more significant than the stress you feel from the trauma. This indicates that dealing with stress requires conquering trauma. For most people. Trusted Source, the consequences of trauma, such as increased anxiety, fade over time. The amount of time required varies greatly. It could take weeks, months, or even years. Anxiety management strategies can be beneficial during the rehabilitation process. The Depression and Anxiety Association of America advises the following methods for having tension and pressure:
1. Limiting drugs that may exacerbate sensations of nervousness such as caffeine or alcohol.
2. To improve sleep quality.
3. prioritize exercise.
4. eat a balanced diet.
5. Learn methods of relaxation (e.g., structured breathing or meditation).
6. Take self-care breaks (e.g., a short walk or enjoying music).
7. celebrate daily accomplishments.
8. Take within humour.

Management for trauma and anxiety
Although not everyone needs therapy regarding trauma and anxiousness, it is always always to a counsellor or psychologist about your concerns. If your symptoms make it difficult for you to go about your everyday activities, you should seek professional help. Engaging with a therapist might help you comprehend what you've experienced. Even if you don't have a trauma-related disorder, recuperation will assist you recover from an awful occurrence quickly.
If you deal with trauma-related chaos, starting with PTSD, your formalized course of action may include particular methods of therapy and drugs. Typically, mental health practitioners use cognitive behavioural therapy (CBT) frameworks to address trauma.
These approaches emphasize the remodelling of problematic thought and behaviour patterns, as well as the gradual, planned encounter with worry and other unpleasant emotions.
Common cognitive psychological methods in trauma therapy consist of Long-term exposure to medical care. The cognitive processing method is trauma-focused. CBT group therapy. A mental health specialist may recommend medication for depression, sleep aids, or anxious counsellors, as well as other medications, to assist you in controlling signs that are immediately debilitating or disturbing.

Conselling

Trauma and anxiety are related to your body's natural stress reaction, as well as changes in the way the brain works that occur after trauma. While many people may not require therapy for trauma-related anxiety, communicating with a counsellor or psychiatrist can help in recovery. When trauma-related anxiety leads to an anxiety-related condition such as PTSD, comprehensive therapy with counselling and drugs may be required.

Always Looks For a Way To Make
Yourself Happy, that's another great
way to surpass Overthinking

CHAPTER EIGHT

HOW TO IMPLEMENT MINDFULNESS TO STOP OVERTHINKING?

Being mindful is the discipline of directing one's energies on the current situation without criticism. It has been demonstrated to have quite a few wellness advantages, including anxiety and depression reduction, relationship improvement, and increased general wellness.

Listed below are some basic methods to nurture concentration in everyday life: Take a few moments each day to sit peacefully and meditate on your inhalation and exhalation. Take note of the warmth of your airflow as it flows in and out of your entire system. If your mind starts to roam, carefully redirect them back to the breath.

Pay close interest in how you feel. Spend a few minutes focusing on what you observe, sense, taste, smell and touch. Consider every feeling in your system as you interact with the environment around you.

Practice thankfulness. Take a couple of seconds every morning to meditate on what you are thankful for. This might include huge things like your wellness or loved ones, as well as small pleasures like the sun or a wonderful meal. Use mindfulness to manage stress. When you start to feel stressed out take a few long breaths and concentrate on the present. Take note of the way you feel and think, but resist the need to let them consume you completely. Instead, aim to view things objectively. Implement mindfulness throughout every aspect of your life. Whether you're tidying the utensils or heading for a stroll, try putting your entire keenness on the activity at hand. Take in everything that is part of this very moment. Consciousness assists you in communicating with greater efficiency. Pay watch over the phrases you use and how you communicate with others. Consider any rulings or assumptions you may be creating, and attempt to speak with an open and interested mind. Conduct eating mindfully. Take your time with your meals, focusing on their aromas and perceptions. Stop consuming food when you're full, instead of eating out of repetitive behaviour.

Release yourself of any worry or anxieties and do your best to clear your thoughts. Integrate mindful living into everyday activities. Pick one or two thoughtful actions per day, such as taking a bath or washing your teeth.

Find a way of life that is productive for you. There are multiple techniques for mindful living to select from, such as breathing exercises, yoga, and walking. Explore multiple strategies to identify the option that best suits you. Recall that mindful living is an ability that requires time to develop. Do not give up if you find it challenging at first. With execution, it becomes quicker and more natural.

CHAPTER NINE
FREQUENTLY ASKED QUESTIONS

When is thinking too much beneficial?
The main feature of an introvert is overthinking. It has positive and negative effects, but with proper usage, it may become a huge advantage. It can help you maintain concentration on what you want to achieve. First, it offers you an overview of the possibilities along with how to navigate with it. A lot of people are unaware of how to handle the situation.

Overthinking may result in living for oneself instead of for others, as it keeps your mind focused on your daily tasks. You hesitate to devote time to others.

You don't need others in your space since your intellect is your friend. I'd want to point out that thinking too much permits you to talk to yourself, which is also known as listening to yourself, which can help you realize who you are.

Instead of becoming egoistic, you compete with yourself rather than others, making you feel uncomfortable and humble in social situations. Although it has numerous benefits, it can be tough to move on from a circumstance. So stay cool and don't take anything too seriously. Leaders are often known for their propensity to think too much.

What helps an overthinker?

Overthinking is strongly associated with negative ideas. So when someone has bad thoughts, they begin to overthink for example, you may be wondering what someone else is saying concerning you, or you may be making a choice, and are doubtful if it is the right one.

Solution:

Don't take things personally.

The world is judgmental, but you can't please everyone.

Complaints and problems are often beyond your control.

Be industrious (MOST IMPORTANT) - it allows you to avoid overthinking, and the satisfaction of completing your task will make you feel comfortable as you are not falling behind.

Get to speak up for yourself.

Build Your Confidence.

The influence of peers is also a factor, so start setting boundaries.

CONCLUSION

Remember that today is tomorrow, yet you're concerned about yesterday.

Overthinking is typically a habit that has evolved, and it is not something we can simply turn off overnight. We are overthinking an event that happened in the past, trying to figure out why things occurred or why someone did something, judging someone or a situation, or being upset with someone or something. Similarly, if we overthink anything in the future, it might be defined as obsessively obsessing about specifics while losing sight of the bigger vision.
How does thinking too much influence you?
It hurts how well we feel physically and mentally. It prevents you from being present in what is happening and produces stress and worry! Also, despite all of our fears and tension from overthinking the day before, nothing happened as we expected. It leads to self-doubt. You undoubtedly realize you've gone down the same intellectual route before, but you keep going like you're in a rut. It is a waste of time and effort.

How Can I Quit Overthinking?

Bring yourself into the current situation. In other words, when we overthink, we are unable to be present in the moment. The truth, nevertheless, is that our current situation is frequently significantly superior to the past or future we are obsessively thinking about. Modify your ideas: Yes, you can't regulate the scenarios that run through your head, but you can switch out harmful ideas with healthier ones. Make a minor shift in focus. How frequently have you quit working on a particular issue to take a break? The solution appears in your thoughts half an hour later. Simply getting up from your chair and moving to a distinct room can help. If possible, get outside. Specifically, attempt to take.

Act rather than overthink:

Choose a modest task that you can complete immediately, and then complete it! You may feel more in charge of the circumstances as a result of this.

Take A Break:

Concentrate on the space you are in. Name anything using each of the five senses that you can see, hear, feel, and so on. Carry something with you. Become fully involved in a hobby. Painting, reading, crocheting, and crafting are a few examples. Do whatever interests you. Set a deadline for yourself: You can frequently make wise decisions quickly. Refrain from delaying making a decision longer than necessary. Setting a deadline can help you decide swiftly and effectively. To make up your mind, give yourself a few minutes to many days. Press the trigger, then proceed.

A good decision can often be made very quickly. Avoid taking longer than you need to make a choice. A deadline can be an effective way of making a decision quickly. Give yourself a few minutes to a few days, to make up your mind. Pull the trigger and move on.

To stop exaggerating, adopt meditation. Pay attention to what you are hearing, but avoid putting names to the noises. If your thoughts stray, return them to the noises you are concentrating on. If your mind names the sounds, don't worry or criticize yourself; this is only your mind trying to keep busy. An overthinking mind is never satisfied with its conclusions. Most of the time, we are either anticipating a prospective result, fretting over an event which could happen, or expecting a specific behaviour or result. You can, nevertheless, effectively begin to overthink fewer and fewer times with adequate practice, which will ultimately assist you in stopping overthinking once more.

Be Victorious Over Overthinking